Tracey Williams Presents

Born Out Of The *Fire*

7 Steps To Heal From Family Trauma

Dedication

I dedicate my book in loving memory to my parents, Stanley Richardson, Sr. and Gilda D. Richardson-McCoy. As I wrestled for several years with the unction to write this book my ultimate prayer was, "Lord help me convey this message into the hearts of those who have faced and conquered abuse, trauma, and dysfunction within their families." I thank my Lord and Savior Jesus Christ for the grace to tell my story.

It is with great love and joy, that I honor Pastor Sylvester Williamson, Jr. and his beautiful wife, Gail P. Williamson. After the transitioning of my parents, they promptly stepped up and committed to the journey of parenting, loving, guiding and mentoring me. What an empowering journey it has been! Without your contribution of love, prayer, and consistent words of encouragement – my outcome may have been completely different. Your example of leadership has been exemplary not only in my life but in the lives of many.

Pastor Sylvester and Gail gave me the courage to see the unique purposes this book would serve. They empowered me to confront a topic most families shy away from or choose to "sweep under the rug." This opportunity to share from a place of transparency and pain was my birthing place to help minister to others. It empowered me to courageously confront the topics people would rather suppress. Prayerfully, my passion to convey this heartfelt message will liberate many from their emotional imprisonment.

I dedicate this book to every person who has survived the trauma of their past, the pain of their family, and the voices of dysfunction. The deadly trio of family abuse, trauma and dysfunction can leave one emotionally, psychologically and mentally crippled. The "deep dark" family secrets have often left many paralyzed in their pain. Today, I am a testament that your courage to share is necessary so that someone else can heal.

To every reader, I applaud your bravery. I honor you because you made a conscious decision not to just survive but to overcome. You are an overcomer. You are a chain-breaker. You are a beacon of light and a voice of hope. You are a voice of justice. You are a bell of freedom ringing and will continue to ring loudly in someone's future. They too will heal, overcome and love again because you had the courage to share your story.

I take this opportunity to honor and thank my husband Alfonzo M. Williams, Sr. for his endless prayers. Babe, you have truly been my "birthing coach" throughout this entire labored process. You have watched me war, cry, laugh, and spin out of control some days. You have graciously felt the blows of my highs, lows and everything in between. Throughout this journey, you have been my faithful intercessor, my constant source of strength and my laughter during the times I wanted to cry. I truly love and honor you.

Briona, David and Michael you have been the wind beneath my wings on many days. Your smiles, jokes, prayers, and counseling/encouragement sessions made all the difference in my world. It is for your freedom and your children's freedom that I write this book.

To everyone reading my story, "Born Out Of The Fire," may you experience God's unconditional love, healing power and amazing grace as you take this journey to freedom with me.

Foreword

My mother and father had three children, I am the oldest and only daughter. My mother was the second oldest out of eight, which consisted of six girls and two boys. My aunts were always loving, smart and the stabilizing force of the family. At the opposite end of the spectrum was my father, an only child with a father who was a travelling salesman and a mother who decided that being a wife and mother was not for her. So she left tragic, dramatic and true.

All his life my dad longed for a semblance of a family, and upon their marriage he wholeheartedly embraced my mother's family as his own. Family has always been important to me and I have never been one to refer to anyone outside of my family as a relative – that is not until I met Tracey Richardson. You see in 1996, Tracey Williams had not yet married the love of her life. She was Tracey Richardson.

I met Tracey while attending a Scripture-based weight loss class. Attending the class with me was my best friend, Earlene. While Earlene and I were friends when we started, a friendship developed between Tracey, Earlene, and myself as we progressed through the class. After our weekly class, we often stayed longer catching up on the events that had taken place since the previous week and praying. What started as a common goal to lose physical weight developed into a relationship in which we were able to *lay aside every weight and the sin that so easily beset us* (Hebrew 12:1).

It was during this time that I had the thought that I was to be a mother to Tracey. Can you imagine my alarm as I realized that the Lord was directing me to be a mother to someone that I did not give birth to? But I could not deny His unmistakable voice. Later I would learn, from Tracey, that the Lord had told her that I was a mother to her.

In the 22 years since we first met, I have come to understand that a family goes beyond the physical lines of relationship. A family, (as defined by Merriam-Webster) is not just those that share common ancestry but also includes "a group of people united by certain convictions or a common affiliation: FELLOWSHIP."

What began as a common desire to change our appearance grew into a relationship and fellowship ordained by the Lord. Tracey and I have shared our love for the Lord and for His Word; we have cried, grieved, rejoiced, prayed, worshipped and loved each other. We have laughed at private jokes – just mention "ashes to ashes" to Tracey and watch her reaction! Our families have eaten, prayed, and mourned together. My husband and I have the honor of being one set of grandparents to Tracey's sons.

I have been a witness to the miraculous transformation that has taken place in Tracey's life. As a mother watches the growth of her child, I look at Tracey and say, this is the Lord's doing and it is marvelous in my eyes! Tracey has been Born Out Of The Fire!

Minister Gail P. Williamson
National Church of God

Table of Contents

Born Out Of The Fire

Message To The Reader

I n this book, I am extremely transparent about my journey of disappointment, pain, fear, and insecurities. I am excited to share with you the amazing love of God and His great power to heal and transform my life. We often hide our pain because of shame, pride and even guilt. I decided to allow my journey to transform me into a messenger of God's hope.

As God began to impress upon my heart to share some of my journey, He revealed that my story would help those suffering in silence. I pray that my story will allow you to find peace. May you discover the unconditional love to heal the broken pieces as you embrace the courage to walk through the fire and allow God to refine you.

God's unconditional love gives us the healing and power to share our journey with others. Now is your time to heal and live a life of love and freedom. God loves you and will never allow your past trauma, abuse or dysfunction to define you. He calls you blessed! His plans are to prosper you and give you an amazing future!

You are Born Out Of The Fire!

Born Out Of The Fire

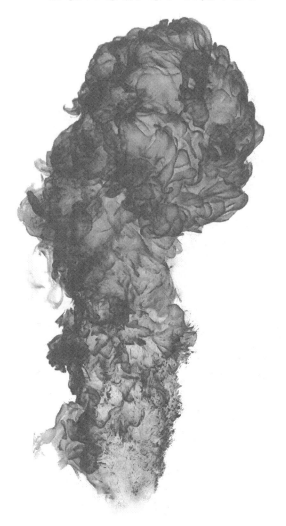

Introduction

For thou, O God, hast proved us: thou hast tried us, as
silver is tried. Thou hast caused men to ride over our
heads; we went through fire and through water: but
thou broughtest us out into a wealthy place.

-PSALMS 66:10,12 KJV

In the fire is where miracles happen. What is a miracle, you ask? I am. My life is a miracle. The definition of a miracle is an unusual or wonderful event that is caused by the power of God. Unusual? Wonderful? That is a clear contrast of how my life began and presently is. I was born out of the fire!

You made all the delicate, inner parts of my body and
knit them together in my mother's womb. Thank you
for making me so wonderfully complex! It is amazing to
think about. Your workmanship is marvelous—and how
well I know it. You were there while I was being formed
in utter seclusion! You saw me before I was born and
scheduled each day of my life before I began to breathe.
Every day was recorded in Your book! How precious it is,
Lord, to realize that You are thinking about me con-
stantly! I can't even count how many times a day Your
thoughts turn toward me. And when I waken in the
morning, You are still thinking of me!

-PSALMS 139:13-18 TLB

I was born to Stanley and Gilda Richardson, at DeWitt Army Hospital in Ft. Belvoir, VA on November 26th at 3:13 am. I am the only girl of six children. I was destined to be a fighter for sure. My name, Tracey, with its British origin, means "war-like" or "fighter." It certainly prophesied my destiny before I made my grand entrance into the world! My father, Stanley Richardson, Sr. was a wounded, Purple Heart recipient. My mother, Gilda Davis, was a young and scared teenage mom. At the age of four, my Momma led me in a prayer to receive Jesus Christ as my Lord and Savior. They believed their baby girl would be great and live a life of impact.

The devil's attempt to kill always begins in the "seed" stage. Trauma, rejection, and abandonment often impacts homes, families, and communities. If we keep the faith and withstand the fire the greatest miracles will transform our lives. God will always be with us as we walk through the fire! What was meant to destroy me ultimately worked in my favor and birthed my testimony to deliver many.

As you enter the flames of life the fire will be uncomfortable and intimidating. However, you will never get burned! Being born out of the fire breeds questions we desire answers for, but all too often receive silence. I realized the fire was a place needed in order for me to release the baggage of my past. It is often hard to unload those bags when you have become accustomed to carrying the weight. Thanks be to God for His great love and His unlimited power to break generational curses and cycles.

God will faithfully carry us through the fire as He births us into our greatest victories! The person we become in the journey brings Him glory and demonstrates His power and love for us.

> *But thanks be to God, who gives us the victory through our Lord Jesus Christ.*
> ~I Corinthians 15:57 Nkjv

Born Out Of The Fire

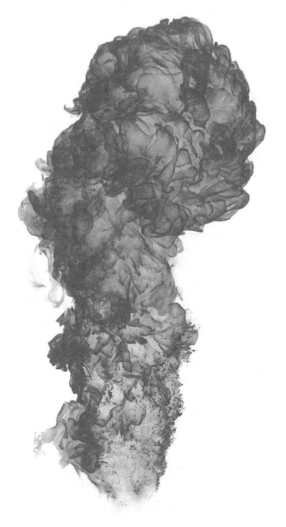

Rejection And Abandonment

Even if my father and mother abandon me,
the Lord will hold me close.

—PSALMS 27:10 NLT

I s it possible for one to be emotionally abandoned and rejected from the womb? I believe it is very possible. You can imagine the rage my father felt when he discovered my mother's secret plot to abort me. Her conniving, calculating mind convinced her that she could successfully murder me without his consent or knowledge – and get away with it. Her choice had nothing to do with their love or marriage. It was the pitter-pattering of Stanley, Jr. moving through the house and the judgmental voices of her mother and mother-in-law ringing loudly in her ears. This was enough for Momma to easily accept her decision. The power of influence in one's mind can cause them to do just about anything.

How often do we allow the negative influences, voices of our past and our bloodline dictate decisions we know to be wrong? An abortion? My mother was nineteen years old, married and prepared to ABORT my life. The unexpected and unwanted pregnancy set the stage for the rejection and abandonment, I felt from my mother. There was always the nagging sense of knowing that my mother loved and favored my older brother over me. After all, I was more like my Father and my brother was more like my mother. I often believed my mother was jealous of the relationship I had with my dad. The place I held in his heart was undeniable. If anyone would ask my dad if I was his baby girl his face would light up like a beam shining brightly. He would always answer,

"Yes that's my baby girl!"

I often questioned why couldn't my mother feel the same way. I was left with a hole in my heart knowing that my mother cared for my brother more than me. I knew my mother didn't love me the same; however, I still loved, respected and honored her.

Have you ever felt like you were that sibling who wasn't loved like everyone else? Did the emotional abandonment leave you with a sense of being unwanted and unloved? If you answered Yes, I have good news! God specializes in loving the unloved, rejected, abandoned and overlooked.

This is the Lord's doing and it is wonderful to see.
—Psalms 118:22, 23 NLT

God uses those who are rejected to accomplish His will and demonstrate His power in their lives.

Before I entered the world Satan used rejection and emotional abandonment to cripple my feelings and handicap my ability to receive love. I was birthed into the fire struggling for acceptance, love and the need to prove my worth. Every little girl yearns for her mother's love. As a little girl, I never knew what it truly meant to feel the true measure of my mother's love. The need to feel her love was more vital to me than the very air I needed to breathe in order to exist. The absence of her love left me struggling to escape the flames burning deep down on the inside of me as I gasped for air.

Having a mother's love would have allowed me to feel safe.

Instead, I was left feeling vulnerable, unprotected and uncovered. The raw emotions of loneliness were more than I could bear. I often wondered did my mother love me for being the very offspring of her and my father's love? Would she ever teach me the lessons of life every mother teaches her daughter? I would never know.

My mother had her own pain to navigate and demons to fight. She was constantly waging war within herself as she suffered with depression and suicidal thoughts. My mother often felt it was more painful to live than to just embrace the cold arms of death. I was left wondering why my mother felt so much pain. The thought plagued my life. I often asked God night after night why as the tears streamed down my cheeks and onto the pillow? I could feel a sense of evil, darkness and despair plaguing my home. In fact, at night I felt its presence suffocating me. The evil spirits sucked the very hope out of my home.

What happened over the next few days was beyond what I could have imagined. Watching my Mother's erratic behavior gave me chills and an eerie feeling that plagued the deepest parts of my soul. The gaze I saw in her eyes was like looking into a pitch-black room expecting to see what was present. I can remember times when I would call out to my mother and she was always responsive. However, on this day she was unresponsive. More like a zombie. She was closed up in her room for hours unresponsive to my calls. I decided to go upstairs and check on her only to find her curled up on her bed in a fetal position with the blinds closed so tight only a hint of sunlight shined through the blinds. I went back downstairs feeling confused and afraid.

My worries came to an end when I heard footsteps coming down the stairs. It was my mother; however, the look on her face horrified me. Nothing could prepare me for what I was about to experience. My mother proceeded to lie down on the living room floor. She called me over so I kneeled down beside her. She opened her hand and placed the butcher knife that she was gripping over her loudly beating heart and placed my hand over top of the knife. She removed her hand and left the knife clenched in my hand. She uttered the words no eight year old girl should ever hear her mother say,

"Tracey stab me in the heart."

Those chilling words rippled through the air and gripped my heart. Everything within me knew what she was asking me to do was wrong. My heart was filled with fear. There was no way I was going to stab my mother. She tried to assure me that God would forgive me because I was a child. I refused to stab my mother. I dropped the knife and kicked it away from us. I said,

"No, Mommy I'm not going to kill you. I am going to pray that God takes away all the pain you are feeling."

The fear I felt as I kneeled over my mother in the living room left me feeling tormented, paralyzed, and haunted.

Can you imagine your mother asking you to end her life? Realizing I was not going to help her she left the knife on the floor and ran up stairs. Her eyes were filled with tears. I heard the door close and through the walls the sound of deep cries pierced the air. My heart was filled with sorrow. I was eight years old. What was I to do? I was left with so many unanswered questions, "Could a mother's pain be so deep that she would summon her daughter to end her life? Could the pain of her past trauma leave such an indelible mark on her soul?" My mother was left trying to escape the pain she was feeling, make sense of the emotions she was dealing with and salvaging it all while raising her children and being a good wife.

At the age of eight I learned that pain, abuse and trauma could be passed down from generation to generation. Also, I learned that neither suicide nor murder was a way of escaping pain. At some point in the family bloodline, someone must rise and say, "Enough is enough!" I believe in my heart, at the tender age of eight, something stood up inside of me, like a mighty defender and declared, "Enough is enough!" My children will never have to go through this.

That chilling episode in the living room was only a precursor for what was to come. The blustery, bitter cold winter had passed and the fragrant, blossoming, rebirth of spring was ushering in the long-awaited summer. Instead of enjoying family trips to the beach, long walks in the evening, playing in the park, we were left to guard, protect, and watch over our mother. She spent the summer in severe depression and the entire family was on suicide watch. The tormenting duo had returned (suicide and depression). The summer of 1978, two years earlier, my mother swallowed an entire bottle of pills as she attempted to take her own life. The deadly duo was waging and contending war for her soul. My mother laid in bed and slept for days and months, without a desire to live.

I remember my Dad had to travel out of town and deliver some vehicles for his job. He had no idea what was to come. My mother left my oldest brother and I alone in our end-unit townhome without any adult supervision. She instructed her nine and eight year old children not to answer the door or the telephone for any reason. As if we were old enough to really understand what she was asking of us. She left us home alone terrified with no one to protect, guard, or make us feel safe. I felt alone. All I had was the vow of my nine-year-old brother that he would protect us. He said,

> "Don't worry about it, Baby Sis. I won't let anything happen to you, okay?"

I held on to the vow of his words as my protection. The entire week we stayed home from school. As the week came to an end, we were running out of food. My brother stood on a box and cooked us grits for breakfast, lunch, and dinner. Thank God we did not starve. However, our souls were starving from the feeling of abandonment. Filled with the horror of our parents never returning neither physically nor emotionally. I stopped daydreaming, believing and feeling.

Filled with worry my thoughts were interrupted by the sound of the doorbell. Immediately, we both panicked as we felt a sense of relief. I know Mama told us not to answer the door or the telephone, but I ran to the door in hopes that my mother or father had come back for us. I opened the door and there stood a man with a bag of groceries. My brother and I were so happy. I thought to myself, how did he know we needed food? How did he know the cabinets were empty? How did he know we were all alone with no sign of Mommy or Daddy? I grabbed the bag and ran to put it on the dining room table. I was so excited to know we would have enough food to eat until my parents returned. I ran back to the door to thank the man, I looked to the left, I looked to the right, and there was no sign of him. I just wanted to say thank you and express how grateful I was for his act of kindness. The Bible instructs us to be careful when we entertain strangers, because some have been in the presence of angels and were unaware. I believe that day an angel visited to drop off food for us to eat.

The angelic visitation on that Friday afternoon gave me

hope. I was still very much afraid. I missed my parents. I just wanted one of them to show up and comfort us. Although only six days had passed, it felt like eternity. It was Saturday morning and the bright, red numbers on the digital clock read 9:57 a.m. I heard the sound of keys in the door and it was my father. I didn't know whether I should run down the steps to greet him or lie in my bed and pretend to be asleep as if this past week never happened. I leaped out the bed, ran down stairs and jumped into his arms, hugging his neck as tightly as I could. Daddy, I'm so glad to see you! He laughed and asked me,

"Girl, why is your hair so nappy? Your momma didn't do your hair today?"

I loosened my grip of the bear hug and my eyes dropped to the floor and in a small voice, I said, mommy is not here. He asked,

"What do you mean mommy is not here?"

With a sigh of relief, I told him, we've been here by ourselves all week. Mommy left after you left for work on Saturday. I glanced at my brother who was silently wiping his tears as well. Deep inside our young hearts, we did not want to get our mother in trouble. Although we were left unprotected, there remained yet still a sense of loyalty within us that we needed to protect her. I felt it was necessary to tell my father what happened during the incident in the living room. After uncontrollably sobbing, gasping for air and wiping my swollen eyes, I began to recount the incident of the butcher knife with him. As he took a seat on the couch, Daddy kept saying,

"Are you all okay? Are you okay, Tracey?"

I am fine, Daddy. I'm just so happy that you are home and with me. We spent the evening taking turns sitting on Daddy's lap and talking with him about everything we could think of. From that day forward, Daddy never went out of town without taking us with him.

Every void I felt, every tear I cried that week, every bad dream I experienced seemed to all melt away into the distance at the very presence of my father. He calmed fears in me and made the raging seas of my emotions, mind, and heart be still. The assurance of his presence made me feel safe and secure again. I no longer worried about the next meal, the knocks on the door, or the endless ringing of the telephone. My daddy was home.

Jesus promised in His word that He would never leave us nor forsake us. He promised He would always be with us, even until the end of the earth and until the end of this age. That promise became a reality to me as a young child as I prayed for my parents. I would always remind Jesus of His promise to never leave me alone.

It was Sunday evening and momma finally came back home. Her eyes were puffy and it looked as if she had been crying for days. She spoke as she walked past us in the living room and headed straight upstairs to her bedroom. My heart was pounding at the speed of lightening! Daddy had just got out of the shower. The arguing and yelling between my parents began. Now that momma was home, my dad wanted to go out with his friends and brothers that evening. I heard thumping, furniture moving and momma yelling:

"You ain't going nowhere Stanley!"

When I looked up from styling my doll baby's hair, my father was standing at the top of the stairs fully dressed. He had everything on except his shoes. He proceeded to walk down the steps when momma jumped on his back! My mother was 5'2" and weighed about 115 pounds. My father was 6'0" and weighed about 230 pounds. With my mother hanging on to my father his feet slipped and they both came tumbling down the stairs. At the bottom of the stairs sat our floor model television. My mother landed at the bottom and hit her head on the corner of the TV. Her head began to bleed. My father yelled,

"What is wrong with you Gilda? You are just as crazy as you want to be!"

My brother and I sat on the couch hugging each other tightly with tears streaming down our faces. My emotions were raw and my mind confused as we helped our bloody mother up off the floor. Despite the blood streaming from my mother's head, my father stormed out and slammed the door.

The events that occurred that week left an indelible scar upon my emotions, my heart, my mind, and my soul. I forgave my mother. At the age of eight, I learned to forgive quickly. Anger and unforgiveness can leave one feeling like a caged bird, which desires only to spread its wings and fly, and experience the freedom of love, joy and peace. When I refused to forgive, I found that I slowly became that which I hated. I refused to be an inmate in the cell of unforgiveness counting days and offenses, while recalling the hurt of all the wrongs done to me.

Unforgiveness has a way of imprisoning one and leaving them chained to their emotions, hurtful experiences, and offenders. God teaches us lessons on the principle of forgiving others. God teaches us in His word that we must forgive others in order to receive His forgiveness.

> *"Shouldest not thou also have had compassion on thy fellow servant, even as I had pity on thee? And his lord was wroth, and delivered him to the tormentors, till he should pay all that was due unto him. So likewise shall my heavenly Father do also unto you, if ye from your hearts forgive not every-one his brother their trespasses."*
>
> —MATTHEW 18:23-35 KJV

Ask yourself: "Are you tormented in your mind? Are you tormented in your soul? Are you tormented in your sleep?" I challenge you to search your heart and mind to discover the answers. Pray and ask God the question, "Who do I need to forgive?" Forgiveness was the key that opened the doors of my emotional imprisonment. I am now free of all offenses and offenders. The day I decided to own my freedom, I learned to forgive and love those who disappointed, betrayed, and offended me. My mother taught me a great lesson in forgiveness that I will carry with me for years to come. When you forgive you gain the power to break the emotional chains of rejection and abandonment.

Step 1 Forgiveness from the Heart

Take a moment and ask the Holy Spirit to give you the names or show you faces of those you need to forgive. List their names below:

1._____

2._____

3._____

4._____

5._____

Prayer of Forgiveness

"Heavenly Father, I come to you seeking release from the emotional prison of unforgiveness and torment that I have been living in for far too long. The anger and bitterness that I carry has kept me from forgiving those whom I have named.

Today, I acknowledge that forgiveness is by faith and not by my feelings. I ask that You remove all unforgiveness from my heart and give me the strength to forgive and release the offenses and those who have offended me. I ask you God to unleash me from the emotional chains that have me imprisoned to the bondage of unforgiveness. In my prayer of release, I pray that You would heal and restore the brokenness within my family, relationships and friendships. Today, I make the choice to forgive from my heart all offenders, in Jesus name. Amen."

Born Out Of The Fire

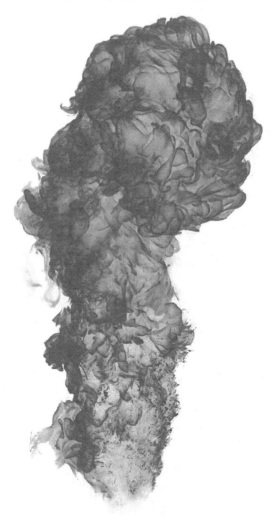

Trauma To Triumph

He heals the brokenhearted and binds up their wounds.

—Psalm 147:3 esv

Trauma, whether emotional, psychological or physical is said to damage the mind, body and soul. It is normally the result of a severely distressing life event. Which often results from an overwhelming amount of stress that exceeds one's ability to cope or handle the emotions involved from that traumatic experience.

Some effects trauma has on children are:

- It can affect children's mood and their ability to regulate their emotions (easy to upset but extremely hard to calm down)
- It can cause numbness to emotions
- It can affect their eating and sleeping habits (some may experience nightmares)
- It can cause isolation; which often makes it difficult to ask adults for help
- It can cause increased difficulty in learning and paying attention

If left untreated, the effects of trauma can last a lifetime.

The effect of trauma often extends beyond childhood and into adulthood. Adults are often left with the emotions, memories, and anxiety of a traumatic experience that occurred in their life. Trauma can leave one feeling numb, disconnected, and unable to trust other people. When bad things happen, it can take a while to get over the pain and begin to feel safe again. Often leaving your sense of security shattered. Whether knowingly or unknowingly people are living with wounds caused by trauma.

From the age of 4-7, I was rambunctious, energetic and full of life. I was outgoing and I enjoyed going to school. My teachers loved me because I was always eager to help my class-mates, once my work was completed. I was a born leader full of fire. I attribute my tenacity to my parents for raising me to be independent, confident and a child of God. My parents raised me in church and taught me how to love God from a young age. They taught me the importance of having my own relationship with God. I enjoyed going to church every week, because I loved singing in the choir. We would travel to differ-ent churches and I would sing my little heart out for the Lord. I looked forward to Sunday mornings attending Sunday school and seeing my friends from church. Did I mention my Father was a licensed Minister who loved to travel and preach the gospel of Jesus Christ? At a young age, my parents taught me that one of the most effective disciplines was the importance of having prayer in my life. They always reminded me that no matter how young I was God could hear my prayers and that He would always answer them.

I can only imagine what happened to the happy little girl who enjoyed going to school, church and helping others? Not understanding why, at the age of eight I began to morph into a quiet, shy, reserved and sad little girl. I had no idea what it meant or felt like to deal with the effects of trauma. I slipped into a dark tunnel that I created within and only emerged when

I pretended to function in life. I found it difficult to be out-going and make new friends at school. My way of coping was pretending my life was normal. I went from being an outgoing girl to one who no longer knew the sound of her voice. Trauma has a way of silencing your voice.

My voice was lost at the age of eight the day my mother tried to convince me to end her life. Left traumatized and con-fused my view of life was distorted. My entire sense of secu-rity was shaken to the core. I believe that was the moment the door of insecurity opened in my life. I was left feeling helpless, numb, paralyzed and disconnected from reality. The trauma of the incident stripped my sense of safety and left me feeling exposed and vulnerable. If my own mother did not value her life who was going to teach me to value mine?

I found myself being afraid to be home alone with my Mother. The memory of that day would forever be etched in my mind. To cope, I would come home from school and go straight to my room to do my homework, pray and read my bible. My bible became my daily escape to ease and erase the pain I was feeling. Reading the stories of Jesus healing the sick, opening the eyes of the blind, and providing food for orphans, widows and their children gave me hope that God would never abandon me. I held on knowing that God loved me. Jesus was so REAL to me. So much so, I would sit in my bedroom and write Him letters. I would tell Him all about my day at school. I would draw pictures for Him. I would even sing Him songs from the Bible verses I read. I would ask Him endless ques-tions. In my heart and mind, He would sit on the edge of my bed and meet me there. Unlike other children, I had no desire to watch television or even play outside. I simply desired to keep our dates and time together and talk about our day. He would say things to make me laugh and even speak words of comfort to me. My daily time with God became my solace. The more we met to talk, the more I began to heal.

My family was falling apart! I was eleven years old and my parents were getting a divorce. In the final divorce the judge granted my father full custody of my brother and me. I began to feel a sense of normalcy again. I would take the bus to school and my father would be waiting to pick me up in the afternoon. Every day when the bell would ring, I would run down the hall, burst through the school doors and eagerly scan the parking lot for my father's red Cadillac. Once I spotted him I would take off running, jump in the car and tell him all about my day; without even taking a breath. The excitement of seeing my father and sharing our daily routine was something I greatly looked forward to. When we arrived home, my Dad would always tell me,

"Take off those school clothes and put on your play clothes."

He would prepare our snack as we shared some family time. Afterwards, he would go to his prayer room and I would go to my bedroom. It was our father/daughter routine. I enjoyed the light-hearted moments and the consistency of these times. I felt secure. Until one day those feelings of security were threatened. Within moments, sadly it all changed. I heard my father yelling my name from his bedroom,

"Tracey! Come here! Tracey! Come here!"

While running down the hall, I yelled, Daddy! What's wrong? What's the matter I whined? When I arrived in his bedroom, my dad was trembling and in a pool of sweat. He was holding his head rocking back and forth. He instructed me to pack as much of my stuff as I could. He said,

"We need to go to Uncle Fred's house."

I could hear him groaning as I ran to my room to pack. My thoughts and emotions were now moving at the speed of lightening and spinning out of control. This meant we were leaving South Carolina and getting on the road to drive to Virginia where my Uncle Fred lived. All I could think about was what on earth was wrong.

Growing up, our parents believed, what happened in our house stayed in our house. Not this time! I tiptoed to the telephone and called my Uncle Fred to let him know something was wrong with my dad. I told him to look out for my father's call because we were on our way to Virginia. I quietly hung up the phone. It was at that time I overheard my father mumbling something about the war. Yes, my father was a Vietnam War Veteran and Purple Heart recipient. Sadly, in the war my father and his troop buddy were in a foxhole fighting the enemy when they got ambushed. My father witnessed his friend get blown up. The memory often tormented him through horrible nightmares. After the war, my father suffered from Post Traumatic Stress Disorder (PTSD). He often cried, wondering why he lived through the war and not his friend. My mother was the only one who could calm him after he awoke from these nightmares. She wasn't there to help this time. I was left to do the best I could.

We are often reminded of trauma through triggers. My father's trigger was his nightmares. He went from speaking about the war, to rambling about his divorce, to the people who hurt him at church. It was as if a volcano was erupting ferociously and the lava that spewed everywhere was a reminder of his past. My dad seemed delirious as we drove to my Uncle Fred's house. It was a blustery night. The wind was blowing and from a distance, I could see the shadow of Uncle Fred's house. When we arrived that night, my father shared with my brother and me that we would be staying. In shock, my heart felt as if it dropped to the bottom of my stomach. I began to feel dizzy and my palms began to sweat. At that moment, a flood of emotions swept over me.

When parents do not heal from trauma, how can they teach their children to be whole? The next day my father was admitted to a mental institution for evaluation, observation and treatment. He underwent treatment for two weeks. I spent the next several weeks praying for his mental health and full recovery. After his discharge, I never lived with my father again. Although I would visit him often, each visit was a sobering reminder of my need for someone to talk to. Back then society placed stigmas on seeking professional help. If you visited a psychiatrist or "shrink" it meant you were "coo-coo" or just outright crazy. I believe we all need counseling.

I sought the professional advice of a licensed social worker to understand the behavior of children who had been abandoned. Rashida shared her expert opinion:

> *"Here you have two children that were left home alone for a week to fend for themselves. In my professional experience, this more than likely wasn't the first time. And there is a strong possibility mental health issues and substance abuse may have been the source of the problem.*
>
> *Some may question the mother's love for her children. And how could the father and/or other family members not have known this was happening. Reality is that there are some individuals who have mental health diagnosis and substance abuse problems that are functioning and have been functioning on a daily basis until something drastic happens. So, the father and extended family may have had no reason to think that these children were not being taken care of. Also,*

it is possible that the mother, out of love, may have thought that leaving the children home was the best option of protecting them and had every intention of returning home.

While dealing with children during my child protective service years of employment, I have found that children will do whatever it takes to stay together. The older sibling(s) usually would take on the parent role. They would make sure that everyone eats and that things ran as normal as it possibly could at home."

—Rashida Daniels-Prather, BSW/QP

Fast forward to my twenties, I still did not fully understand the effect trauma had in my life. My courage to seek professional counseling, played a critical role in fostering my healing. I discovered that I carried the trauma of my past into my adulthood. Once I recognized the soul wounds were real, I was determined to heal. In life we often lose a part of ourselves; therefore it is important that we spend the time to restore and reclaim what we have lost. As I began to find my healing, I gave myself permission to have a talk with the eight-year old girl in me. I took time to affirm to her that:

- The trauma she experienced was not her fault
- You do not have to be ashamed or embarrassed
- I am deeply sorry this happened to you
- You are a very special child and you are loved
- Your broken heart will heal
- You will one day help someone heal their broken heart
- You are strong and brave
- I am proud of you

That conversation allowed me to see all the great plans God had in store for my life.

I began to see and embrace the hope of a different future. I began to attract healthier relationships, my self-confidence rose, and I learned to embrace the opportunities God blessed me with. When my mindset changed, my behavior changed. When my thoughts changed, my outlook on life changed. I no longer felt inadequate or unworthy to receive the blessings God had in store for me. I believed it was my future and my choice. I was determined to make different choices than my family. When I made the choice to heal I moved from *Trauma To Triumph*.

For I know the thoughts that I think toward you, saith the Lord, thoughts of peace, and not of evil, to give you an expected end.
—JEREMIAH 29:11 KJV

Step 2 Choose to Heal

Prayer for Healing

Heavenly Father, I come to you in the name that is above every name, Jesus Christ, the Son of the Living God. Today, I make a choice to heal. Father, I willingly surrender to you every hurt, pain, disappointment, betrayal, trauma and wounds to my soul. I am not a victim of my circumstances. I am victorious through the blood of Jesus Christ. I receive Your healing power flowing through me physically, emotionally, and mentally. Thank You for healing every traumatic thought and memory. I declare today I am healed! In Jesus name I pray. Amen.

Born Out Of The Fire

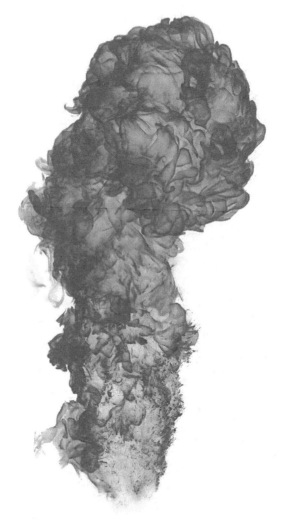

Brokenness To Boldness

He heals the brokenhearted and binds up their wounds.

—PSALMS 147:3 NIV

My spirit was broken. My joy was stripped away. My dreams of the life I had hoped for were officially shattered. While sitting at the kitchen table, staring out the window, I barely noticed the raindrops accumulating on the windowsill. My soul was stuck in a place of confusion and mixed emotions. As I sat there gazing into the unknown while sipping a cup of hot herbal tea, every swallow reminded me just how bitter life can be. It was liberating to daydream as I allowed my mind to drift into the freedom of the unknown. The changes I experienced over the past few years left my mind constantly spinning like a whirlwind.

After my parents separated, every year I would write the same Christmas wish: "That our family would get back together." My family lived on the core value that "No matter what, family should always stick together and look out for one another." After painfully witnessing my parents' 22 year marriage end in divorce, I experienced the highs and lows of what it meant to be part of a family filled with brokenness. The pain I felt from the dysfunction left lasting internal marks I thought I would never escape.

Every child looks to their family as the anchor that keeps them grounded. A broken heart and shattered emotions caused me at times, to hate the ones I should have loved. Often left feeling broken, hurt, confused and worthless. Searching for answers; however, there seemed to be none. Have you ever felt broken beyond repair? Here I was once again in the exact same place I had been before trying to pick up the pieces of my shattered heart. Could there be a sense to it all? My emotions raged like a blistery storm roaring on the inside. Just when I thought the hurt and brokenness was gone, it returned like a tidal wave sweeping over me. The negative feelings continued to plague my spirit.

The spirit of a man can endure his sickness, but as for a broken spirit who can bear it?
—Proverbs 18:14 NASB

The pain of brokenness can often be unbearable. Nothing hurts more than a broken heart. Broken people are often left questioning, "What caused the brokenness? Who caused the pain?" The causes of brokenness can vastly lead to:

- Separation and divorce
- Parental abandonment
- Broken homes
- Physical abuse
- Sexual abuse
- Broken promises
- Past hurt

We often mask our brokenness in many forms:

- Emptiness
- Anxiety

- Bitterness
- Depression
- Addiction
- Compulsive behavior
- Perfectionism

I am all too familiar with masking my brokenness within the confinement of my perfectionism. You see, I always needed everything to be in order. Whenever things were not perfect, I felt responsible for being the fixer. When you are always striving to be perfect, when perfection doesn't exist you will never be able to live up to your own expectations. I believed the reward of my perfection came from the approval, acceptance and love of others. My healing started when I realized that my need to be perfect was a reflection of the love I had for myself. I knew that in order to truly experience healing I had to ask myself some gut-wrenching questions. The answers revealed that it was important for me to stand in my truth and commit to defining life on my terms.

I soon learned my brokenness was not beyond God's healing power and his ability to use me. Without God's help, I would have never been able to lift myself up from such a deep space of pain. My darkest hours became my most memorable times of fellowship with God. It was during that time that I learned to abandon my will and surrender to God's will. I stopped allowing my brokenness to define me. With humility, I brought all my worries, fears and anxiety to God. I knew that I had neither the fortitude nor wisdom to put the shattered pieces of my wounded heart and soul back together. I needed God's true guidance in my life.

We often turn our pain into what we deem as temporary relief. A defining moment was when I realized that temporary numbing was not a substitution for lasting pain. The temporary relief continued to entangle me within the confinement of hopelessness, brokenness and low self-esteem. Some substitutions people use to temporarily numb their pain are:

- Drugs
- Gambling
- Alcohol
- Sex

Ask the drug user who has come down from a high. Ask the gambler who spent their entire paycheck and must face their loved one. Ask the alcoholic who indulges in liquor to soothe the pain. These substitutions have no transformative power; in fact they temporarily numb the wounds. Our deepest desire should be to live a whole life spiritually, physically and mentally.

During my season of healing, it was important to me to discover ways to minister to others in pain. It helped me shift my focus from selfish to selfless. There were days when the pain was all consuming. It caused me to hide from others, wallow in self-pity while warding off depression and suicidal thoughts. People who have been healed from brokenness can identify with people who are broken. They minister from a "no judgement zone" because they understand pain.

Helping others in need allowed me to realize I was not broken beyond repair. I had to trust that God could use even me as one of His servants. I volunteered to help at church crusades and community outreach events. I looked forward to serving and feeding the hungry in the community. I would just smile as I handed them their plate and drink. I often wondered what led people to experience being displaced and homeless. What brokenness had life taken them through? Often while volunteering they would share their story of what led them to that place.

The circumstances often varied:

- Divorce
- Unemployment
- Incarceration
- Tragedy
- Financial Burden of caring for an elderly loved one

Life has no warning signs of when normalcy will take a turn. I was grateful that God made me a bridge of hope for others.

Their boldness to share their stories gave me the courage to begin sharing my story. Some would laugh and say: "Oh! You are a fiery, little preacher girl and you definitely have a story to tell." Those very words unlocked a revelation within me. I realized the most impactful keys to my healing was the power I possessed in my voice. My words packed a punch not of pain but of power. What are you speaking over your life? Are your words filled with life or death? We all have family abuse, trauma and dysfunction to overcome. We must remind ourselves that we are not in the fight alone.

What you say can preserve life or destroy it; so you must accept the consequences of your words.
—PROVERBS 18:21 GNT

I became intentional with my words whether good or bad. I paid careful attention to my conversations and even what I allowed others to speak over me. I realized it was up to me to encourage myself. I would look teary-eyed into the mirror and say: "Tracey it will not always be this way. You will not always suffer from hurt. You will not always feel broken. You will heal and then help others to heal." When I utilized the power of speaking positive words over myself things began to manifest in my life.

As I grew in my identity in Christ, I had to remind myself daily, "I am who God says I am!" God is our Maker. He is our Creator. I realized it was imperative for me to speak the words that God says and believes about me:

- I am the head and not the tail
- I am above and not beneath
- I am fearfully and wonderfully made
- I am more than a conqueror
- I am a lender not a borrower
- I am the righteousness of God
- I am blessed coming in and going out

There is transformative power in speaking words of life to ourselves that will build us up and not tear us down.

Since we have the same spirit of faith according to what has been written, "I believed, and so I spoke," we also believe, and so we also speak.

—2 CORINTHIANS 4:13 ESV

The voices of brokenness and low self-esteem made me believe, I would never be good enough to rise above my circumstances. I replaced the voice of lies within me with words of truth. Oftentimes we do not choose our circumstances or situations; however, we are left to deal with the aftermath. In my journey of healing and deliverance from brokenness, I worked hard to become selfless in all areas of my life. I stopped focusing on self and started serving others. Having the courage to share my story, from *Brokenness To Boldness* helped others. It is a way for others to see beyond where they are to where God will have them to be. Is someone waiting for you to tap into your courage today?

Step 3 Commit Selfless Acts (Serve Others)

Prayer for Unselfeshness

Father God, I come to you in the name that is above every name, Jesus Christ, the Son of the Living God. Today, I ask that you help me to be selfless and not selfish. You committed the most selfless act of all by sending Your Son Jesus to die on the cross for our sins. Heavenly Father, I admit that in the past brokenness and hurt has caused me to be selfish and display self-pity in certain areas of my life. Today, I pray that every opportunity I am given to serve and help others that I will continue to do so. Father God, the joy that I feel in helping others comes from knowing that You continue to bless me. What I have learned in my journey of serving others is that in return I find peace in my healing. I declare all spirits of selfishness are being removed from my life. Give me the heart of a servant, in Jesus name. Amen.

Born Out Of The Fire

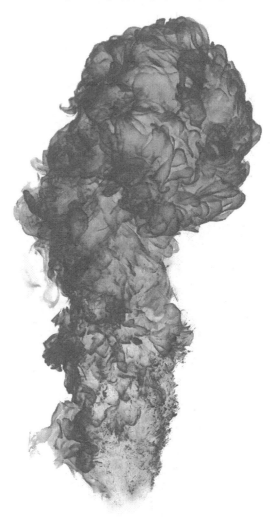

Dysfunction To Dynamic

Every valley shall be filled and every mountain and hill
brought low; the crooked places shall be made straight
and the rough ways smooth.

—LUKE 3:5 NKJV

Our current culture has coined the phrase "dysfunctional family." To some degree, I am sure we can all agree, there are "functioning dysfunctional families." However, I imagine there are some, if not all, longing for healing and searching for remedies to repair the broken pieces of their family. Dysfunction simply implies that behavior which is abnormal, impaired or incomplete in its functioning. In the family structure, it can be a failure to show the characteristics (love, support, encouragement) or fulfill the purposes accepted as normal or beneficial. Normal certainly can be relative as we look at our current family structures.

Perhaps pride and perfectionism causes us to hide our family dysfunction. Is it the need for social acceptance or simply shame? I had to reflect and ask myself the following questions, "Was I ashamed of my family? Was the dysfunctional behavior an embarrassment?" Whatever the reasoning may be, dysfunction has the tendency to appear as the "elephant in the room" that most families shy away from.

At times when we gather as family to enjoy one another, we are faced with unresolved betrayal, past hurt, disappointment and unforgiveness. If these areas are left without resolve they can explode like lava from a seething volcano. We must challenge ourselves to confront the underlying issues and ask the unanswered questions in order to prayerfully reach a resolve. Whatever we are unwilling to confront in our lives ultimately cannot be healed, helped or changed. We must address the unknown, "What will it take to move families from dysfunction to dynamic?" My great grandma used to say,

"Prayer! A whole lot of prayer!"

Historically, family was always known to be the people we could lean on during tough times and rely on and trust wholeheartedly. My maternal great grandmother, Mrs. Mary Brown affectionately known, as "Big Grandma," was the matriarch who kept our spirits lifted and our family glued together. She laid the family foundation and set it in stone. Listen! Big Grandma kept strife to a minimum and encouraged free-flowing family communication during our weekly Sunday dinner gatherings. We could count on family disagreements being resolved over Sunday meals. You could hear the laughter roaring through the house as we fixed our plates, joked with one another and wrestled for the best seats around the television. Big Grandma judged all disagreements fairly and swiftly. When it was over she would say,

"Now go give them a hug and tell them you love them!"

My great grandmother loved inviting me into her kitchen to give cooking lessons. I can remember the sweet aroma that pierced the air whenever my great grandmother was baking her famous triple-decker yellow cake with chocolate frosting. You could smell the sweet fragrance as you walked up to the door. When you entered her home you were greeted with what was sure to make your stomach feel like it was experiencing a taste of heaven on earth. Now she didn't stop at cooking advice. She was sure to share child rearing and relationship advice. At the time, I was a young, single mother. She never failed to give me sound advice on how to prepare to be a good wife when the time would come. Her wisdom was proven and unmatched! And her love was unconditional.

When "Big Grandma" got sick I was devastated. Just when I thought things were looking up and the family was growing closer, my mother advised us that she was admitted to a nursing home. On my initial visit I recall the vast amount of weight "Big Grandma" had lost. Also, I noticed someone had beautified her thinning, grey hair with two beautiful braids. Her hair was longer than I realized. Her once silky, brown skin was now a bit wrinkled. Her protruding veins spoke to me of her life's journey. Not to mention, Big Grandma's combined children, grandchildren and great grandchildren exceeded well over thirty. The love she could feel running through her veins showed through the spark of fire in her eyes. During every visit she managed to offer me a quick smile as she nodded in and out of sleep.

Our visits were always heart-warming before Big Grandma lost her speech. We would joke, laugh and reminisce. She would gladly tell me stories of how bad and rambunctious I was as a little girl. On this visit, she told me her favorite story of how I visited her home one day wearing my favorite brown, plush-velvet coat. I was only four years old and I nicknamed my coat *Bear Brown*. According to Big Grandma, I never wanted to take the coat off! It would always end in a battle of the wills and she would often give in to this little four-year-old. Big Grandma roared with laughter as she recalled the day, I entered the door with my *Bear Brown* coat on and my collar popped. I proceeded to climb onto her coffee table, hands in my pocket and strutted from one end of the table to the other as if I were on a New York runway. I jumped off her coffee table, ran out the front door and joined my cousins in a game of freeze tag as if nothing had happened. I laughed until my side hurt and my eyes were filled with tears. As we continued our conversation, she uttered these profound words,

"Always be dynamic. You got that fire in you girl! Keep the family together because I'm counting on you."

I had no idea why that day she decided to share the very words that would alter the way I viewed my life. That was my last conversation with "Big Grandma" before she passed away.

We lost the matriarch of our family "Big Grandma." As we prepared for the day of her farewell service it was surreal. The funeral was held at Macedonia Baptist Church where my Great Grandmother, faithfully served on the Usher Board for thirty-five years. The home going service was beautiful. My grandmother was a blessing to everyone in my family and the people she came in contact with. As the family marched into the church together and as we walked down the aisle it felt like the longest walk we had ever taken. As we took the opportunity one by one and some in pairs to console one another, we said our final goodbyes to "Big Grandma." As we took our seats the family filled a number of rows with her children, grandchildren, great grandchildren and a host of family and friends. "Big Grandma" was truly the glue that held the foundation of our family together.

During the funeral we leaned on one another for support. With tears streaming down my face, I leaned my head on my cousin's shoulder. He smiled as he tried to comfort all the cousins on the row. My older cousin took his arm and placed it around my shoulder as he began to rub it. For a moment, I felt his touch was more than consolation. I began to ask myself the question, "Was I overreacting? Or should I trust what the butterflies in my stomach were telling me?" I started questioning, "Could this really be happening?" My great grandma always said, "Tracey always go with your first thought or should I say your gut feeling." My gut was telling me that my cousin was rubbing me in an inappropriate way. I didn't know if I was overwhelmed with grief and didn't want to falsely accuse him so I went back to focusing on the service. Never doubt your gut feeling; oftentimes, more than ever you are right.

As the service concluded the family arose from their seats and began to walk down the aisle to exit the church. It was surreal. I realized that would be the last time I would see "Big Grandma." We got in the cars and headed to the cemetery where we concluded Big Grandma's service. From the cemetery we loaded up again to head to the repast. It was amazing to see all the people come out and celebrate the legacy of the woman who truly was the foundation of the woman I am today. My great grandmother was truly loved by everyone because of her faithfulness to her family, church and community.

The day was coming to an end. I was exhausted, overwhelmed and filled with sadness. As we finalized saying thank you and hugging everyone it was finally time to go home. My cousin asked if he could get a ride home because his mother left without him. I agreed but the butterflies in my stomach warned me otherwise. As we were driving to his house, he began to tell me how beautiful I was and that he desired to have a relationship with me. Did I mention we were cousins? In my mind, I thought: "Boy! We are cousins! THAT IS INCEST!" He tried to convince me that our family would accept us being together and no one would care. He thought it was acceptable because my Grandfather, my mother's father, married his first cousin after he and Grandma Dee divorced. How did my Grandfather ever morally convince himself his second marriage would be acceptable in the eyes of family, friends and community? In my mind, heart and soul it was despicable. And I would never perpetuate such a despicable cycle!

The ride was long, awkward and uncomfortable. As we turned onto his street, I began to feel a sense of relief. As we arrived to the house my Aunt met us outside. She said,

"Baby it is too late for you to drive all the way home."

She suggested I spend the night and go home in the morning after a good night's sleep. A little uneasy about what I had experienced on the ride over, I agreed to sleep in the basement. All I could think about was the conversation from the car my mind began to spin out of control.

Finally, I dozed off although; it only felt as if I was asleep for a few minutes when I heard footsteps coming down the stairs. My heart began to race! When I looked up at the bottom step I could see my cousin standing there with a smirk on his face. He continued to make advances at me and then he took it a step further and started touching and caressing me. He kept trying to convince me that what he was doing was ok. Did I mention I was only eighteen years old? I was afraid to scream, because I did not want to awaken my Aunt. Afraid and not sure what to do my palms begin to sweat uncontrollably. My cousin began to get aggressive by pushing himself on me and we began to wrestle. I tried to fight him off with all my might!

Questions began to flood my mind, "Was he going to rape me? Would he be willing to violate me to prove his point and fulfill his lustful passion?" I refused to commit incest. No meant no! I was the only girl of five brothers and I was used to fighting. That night, I was determined to fight and there were no rules when it came to defending myself. I kicked him. I punched him. I grabbed his genitals. I bit him. After what seemed like hours, he finally gave up and retreated upstairs. That night I fought for generations to come to break the curse of incest in my family line. My triumph meant incest stopped with me on that night. The fight was well worth it if it meant moving our family from dysfunctional to dynamic. Big Grandma would have been proud of me.

After he left, I was afraid to sleep. I waited for dawn to peek through the window so I could bid my Aunt farewell and get on the road. I was left with the pondering question, "What kind of family dysfunction was I born into?" At that moment, my heart resonated with King David when he said:

Behold, I was brought forth in iniquity, and in sin my mother conceived me.
—Psalms 51:5 NKJV

After that night, I never saw my cousin again.

Nevertheless, the hope of my healing was not far off. I began to pray and ask God to teach me about the family sins I needed to pray and ask forgiveness for. God began to reveal and open my eyes to signs of dysfunctional traits. These are some of the many patterns and traits in my life that I battled with but overcame with God's gracious help. I realized it wasn't enough to just recognize the traits, so I actively worked to change my dysfunctional thoughts.

In return my behavior changed…

- Abuse – I became a person who would verbally abuse others. My tongue was sharp and my words would cut like a knife. I was not beyond using physical abuse if necessary.
- Addiction – I became addicted to people's approval of me. I wanted people to like me. I did not want people to be mad at me. I became addicted to sex to numb the pain of my wounded soul. I became addicted to material possessions and the need to dress up the outside to hide the internal pain.
- Love with Conditions – I became a person who embraced and lived by performance-based love. As long as one did things to make me happy, they had my love and loyalty. The moment they disappointed me, I would cut them off, cut off all communication and treat them as if they never existed. I had absolutely no problem isolating myself and cutting people off – male or female.
- Lack of Boundaries – I became a person who would go outside the boundaries and break the rules as long as I selfishly achieved what I wanted. I did not have regard for others or consider their feelings. The lines of my boundaries were blurred.
- Poor Communication – I became a person who had extreme challenges expressing my feelings. I would allow things that bothered me to build up inside of me. When I did express myself, it came out through anger and rage. I would later regret how I spoke or treated the individual.
- Fear – I became a fearful individual. I was afraid to open up to new people. I was afraid to love. I was afraid to be

vulnerable. I was afraid to share my pain. I was afraid to trust others—especially women. In the back of mind, I believed everyone would leave me just like my mom did.

God assured me I did not have to repeat these sinful patterns since I became a child of God when I accepted Jesus into my heart.

Therefore, if anyone is in Christ, he is a new creation; old things have passed away; behold, all things have become new.
—2 CORINTHIANS 5:17 NKJV

I believed the prayers for my family could be answered and bring about future change. That day came when I decided the patterns, cycles and behaviors would be broken off my life. I possessed the determination within to become a whole and healed woman. The woman who was once suppressed, suffocated and buried beneath years of abuse, trauma and dysfunction had arisen. One decision moved me from dysfunctional to dynamic. Some days Big Grandma's words rung loudly within me, "Always be dynamic." I often respond to her saying, "It's taking a whole lot of prayer Big Grandma." Today, I am free to love and to be loved.

Step 4 – Commit to Making a Decision

Prayer for Decision-Making

Father God, I come to You, in the precious name of Your Son, Jesus Christ, the Son of the Living God. Today, I make the decision to change. I know it is not enough to recognize the need to change, I must commit to the decision to change. Father, I am asking for Your help in this decision. I am asking You for the strength and fortitude to remain committed to my decision when the journey gets difficult. I cannot do this alone.

Heavenly Father, I make the decision to not be self-reliant, but I place my trust in You. I pray You will seal this decision in my heart today. I pray You remind me of the day I made the decision and commitment to change. Thank You for Your love and faithfulness to me, in Jesus name. Amen.

Born Out Of The Fire

Grace To Change

He has said to me, "My grace is sufficient for you [My loving kindness and My mercy are more than enough—always available—regardless of the situation]; for [My] power is being perfected [and is completed and shows itself most effectively] in [your] weakness." Therefore, I will all the more gladly boast in my weaknesses, so that the power of Christ [may completely enfold me and] may dwell in me.

—2 Corinthians 12:9 amp

My willingness to freely love me opened the doors for me to experience what it meant to accept God's enabling power to grant me the *Grace To Change*. I believe deep within my heart that when I made the choice to change and committed to my decision – grace was there to greet me. Divine grace is available to us all.

Grace can be defined as godly influence operating in our lives. Grace is the loving kindness God shows toward us. It is a magnificent display of His loving, merciful nature. It is the goodness of His nature to divinely help us change when we are simply too weak. Although the desire to change is often present, we lack the needed strength to bring about change. Leading us to places and opportunities where we experience God's grace. I call it "the place of grace." A place where you can find refuge from the weaknesses, failures and insufficiencies that often collide within God's unwavering grace.

Grace is a radiant display of God's loving nature. Grace is God's divine empowerment. Grace has the power to move us from self-reliance to total dependence on God. All too often the world encourages us to rely on the "pull yourself up by your boot straps mentality" that we forget that God's grace is sufficient. When I realized my strength was limited, God allowed me to experience *Grace To Change*. As I fought for my emotional healing and freedom, God revealed that the battle was not mine. It was His to fight. I released control and became totally dependent on God. Letting go of control can often be a struggle; however, I had to make the decision to allow God's grace to guide me. I realized how entrapped I had become from the walls I had built trying to protect and care for myself. Life had tricked me into believing that I was responsible for fighting my own battles. The day I realized it was not my battle but the Lord's, I truly experienced God's grace.

I learned in life that responding to negative circumstances in a dysfunctional way, would never lead to change. I know, by God's grace, what it feels like to experience change. Let me be clear. My healing did not come without going through my demolition season. During that season, I felt vulnerable, stripped, and naked. The family abuse, trauma and dysfunction I experienced left me believing and feeling as if I had to be strong all the time.

I know I am not alone. All too often we put on our *Wonder Woman* or *Superman* cape and believe that we should never show any signs of weakness. We stand on being strong, not only for ourselves, but for everyone connected to us. My brothers and sisters this is true deception. It is in our weakness that God's grace shows itself most effective. Take a minute to ask yourself, am I embracing the *Wonder Woman* or *Superman* mindset? That mindset is a blockage to your healing and deliverance. In today's culture, society promotes the me, myself and I mentality which often leads to destruction. We were never created to struggle alone or suffer in silence. God's grace has been made available to us.

We often hide from the very thing that God is trying to reveal to us. One morning while kneeling and praying God said to me: "It is ok for you to admit to Me that you are weak. It is ok for you to admit to Me that you are tired." At that moment, it was as if God had reached down in the innermost parts of me and released a sob of praise. For the first time in a long time, I felt completely relieved. I had permission to be weak. A great exchange happened that day! I literally felt as if someone had lifted a thousand pounds of weights off my shoulders. I had permission to admit my weariness and allow God to be strong on my behalf. When we are weak – God is strong.

During the demolition phase on my journey to change, I learned how extremely important it was to ask for God's help. For years, I carried needless burdens and weights I did not have to carry. God's grace was available to me. God was just waiting for me to ask.

When the righteous cry for help, the Lord hears and delivers them out of all their troubles. The Lord is near to the brokenhearted and saves the crushed in spirit. Many are the afflictions of the righteous, but the Lord delivers him out of them all.
—Psalm 34:17-19 (esv)

God answers all prayers and every cry for help!

*For it is by believing in your heart that you are
made right with God, and it is by openly declaring
your faith that you are saved. As the Scriptures
tell us, "Anyone who trusts in Him will never be
disgraced." Jew and Gentile are the same in this
respect. They have the same Lord, who gives gener-
ously to all who call on Him. For "Everyone who
calls on the name of the Lord will be saved.*

—ROMANS 10:10-13 (NLT)

Could it be that God is waiting on you today to simply ask
Him for whatever you stand in need of?

When we ask, God answers. What I learned was that I had
to overcome the fear of asking. Once I overcame my fear and
began to ask, it amazed me that the answer was always favor-
ably and gracious to me. Today, I understand that the beauty
of God's grace means that I do not have to struggle in my own
strength. God is a change maker, mind regulator, and a chain
breaker.

*Create in me a clean heart, O God; and renew
a right spirit within me.*

—PSALM 51:10 KJV

Not only will God change you, He will create a new heart
within you.

By God's grace, I see myself differently! One of my favorite
hymns is *"Amazing Grace."* I would always enjoy hearing the
choir sing the lyrics to that song. I believe it is a testament of
God's loving and amazing grace for me. It is a reminder no
matter how empty you feel God's amazing grace will fill your

spirit. The song reminds us that God's grace can erase the feeling of emptiness and restore our sight to see clearly his vision for our lives. Take a minute to pause and look back over your life. I'm sure you're reminded that it was God's loving grace that saved you from life's trials, tribulations, and disappointments. It was God's amazing grace that...

- Saved me from the pain and hopelessness of the fear, sorrow, and brokenness I felt

- Gave me the strength and fortitude to forgive the abuse and hurt I experienced

- Cleansed my heart of all offense, bitterness and unforgiveness

- Broke depression off my life

- Delivered me from suicidal thoughts when voices were telling me I had nothing to live for

- Gave me the validation, approval and value I needed

- Taught me, I am loved and accepted by Him

- Healed my broken heart and assured me I will love again and be loved

God's amazing grace is a reminder that He truly loves me. And He truly loves you no matter how deep your despair may be; His supernatural grace will empower you. His grace cannot be earned. It is freely given to all those who will humble themselves and receive God's amazing grace. God's grace will always be the power to break destructive cycles of the past, launch us into a new life and grant us the *Grace To Change*!

Before ending this chapter, I want to share a story I believe will give insight on God's grace. Let's briefly explore how God's grace reigned in the life of Apostle Paul.

He has said to me, "My grace is sufficient for you
[My loving kindness and My mercy are more than
enough—always available—regardless of the
situation]; for [My] power is being perfected [and
is completed and shows itself most effectively] in
[your] weakness." Therefore, I will all the more
gladly boast in my weaknesses, so that the power of
Christ [may completely enfold me and] may dwell
in me.

—2 CORINTHIANS 12:9 AMPP

In 2 Corinthians 12:1-10, Apostle Paul was dealing with a "thorn in the flesh." Apostle Paul wrote the majority of the New Testament and he was entrusted with beautiful and mighty revelations from the Lord. Yet, his thorn in the flesh was a point of agitation he wanted removed from his life. The scripture does not specifically state what Apostle Paul's thorn in the flesh was; however, it does tell us why the thorn was there – to keep him humble.

Paul pleaded with God THREE times to remove the thorn! God did not. Instead, God promised Apostle Paul that the grace being given unto him was sufficient. Have you ever struggled with that "one thing" in your life? Have you ever prayed: "God! If I could just overcome this one thing then I can handle everything else?" Perhaps God knows our "thorn in the flesh" is the very thing that will keep us dependent on His grace.

The "thorn(s)" in my life left me feeling that if I could only escape the entanglement everything would be fine. I knew I needed God's grace to change my thorns into a work of His beauty. I had to be willing to admit my weaknesses and accept

God's strength. Take a minute to reflect on areas where you need God's grace in your life.

Apostle Paul encountered God's grace on the road to Damascus. My "Damascus Experience" happened in a hospital bed. The hospital room seemed to fade as I heard the doctor say: "I am sorry Ms. Richardson, there is nothing else we can do for you." The first thought that entered my mind was, "Lord, I am a single mother who is going to raise my two-year old daughter?" I was only 25 years old. I desperately needed God's grace. Like Apostle Paul, I had done some terrible things in my life. The same God I turned my back on; ironically, was the first one I thought to cry to in prayer after receiving the news.

Immediately, I telephoned my father and we began to pray. After we hung up, I cried myself to sleep. When I woke up the next day the heaviness I felt the night before was lifted. I remained in the hospital for another five days. Each day I began to feel different. After running tests my doctor entered the room and informed me that all my labs were normal and "strangely" my liver was completely healed!

Like Apostle Paul, God's grace was extended to me. I am so grateful God's love toward us is kind and gracious. He sees the best in us when we are unable to see it ourselves. He loves us unconditionally. I thank God for sparing my life and giving me the *Grace To Change.*

Step 5 – Commit to Asking for Help

Prayer for Help:

Dear Heavenly Father, I come to You, in the precious name of Your Son, Jesus Christ. Like Apostle Paul, my thorns have humbled me. I am in great need of Divine grace. I am in great need of Divine assistance. I cannot work, labor or toil to receive Your grace. I acknowledge it is freely given. Would You exchange my burdens, my weaknesses, my thorns for Your strength today? Heavenly Father, would You lead me to the people You have already assigned to help me? I renounce all forms of fear, intimidation or pride that would prevent me from receiving their help. I willingly and gladly accept help in any form, fashion or method You choose to send in Jesus name. Amen.

Born Out Of The Fire

Breaking Destructive Cycles

And when He had come into the house, His disciples
asked Him privately, "Why could we not cast it out?"
So, He said to them, "This kind can come out by noth-
ing but prayer and fasting."

—Mark 9:28, 29 NKJV

All too often we hear the cliché "old habits die hard." I personally believe children are a product of their environment. We all have learned behavior from our childhood, which shape our worldviews and influence our perspective causing us to develop unhealthy mindsets that we carry with us into adulthood. Breaking destructive cycles takes work and requires patience.

I never imagined spending time with family at Christmas would cause me to later need to break destructive cycles. Every Christmas after opening our gifts at home, we would head over to Grandma Dee's house. I was always excited and anxious to see my cousins. So we could ride our new bikes or zoom down the street with our brand new big wheels, or roller skates. We didn't have a care in the world. Joy was in the air! After all, it was Christmas; the most wonderful time of the year.

Every year at Christmas we gathered for our traditional family dinner to open gifts and curl up and watch movies until late into the evening. Was it me or did the boys always get the best gifts from Grandma Dee? As I got older the gifts became less exciting, I remember one Christmas only receiving socks and a nightgown. While the boys, received the latest electronics. They were excited while my heart sank in disappointment. Of course, I smiled, said "thank you" and pretended to be thankful for my gift. Has this ever happened to you? I can hear you now saying yes!

Watching the excitement on everyone's faces when they received their gifts taught me that people appreciate you when you give them something special. So I believed that buying gifts for people would guarantee their love and approval. Fast-forward to my adulthood when it was time for Christmas I would rush to the mall and shop for lavish gifts for my family. I didn't understand that genuine love and respect could never equate to an amount or be measured in material things. Every Christmas, I went into debt buying endless gifts for my family. I repeated this cycle yearly in hopes that I would gain my family's love and approval. I realized the behavior I had adapted was a destructive cycle I had to break.

When you set out to seek the approval of others you will always have a void that can never be filled. Why you ask? If the people you are seeking approval from does not give you what you need you will often be left feeling inadequate. My need for validation, affirmation and people's approval led me to make bad decisions in my life. My need to feel love from other people made it difficult for me to function when the love I gave was not reciprocated. My need to please others through gifts continuously left me to recover from financial debt and emotional bankruptcy. I was left questioning, "What's wrong with me? Why didn't my family love me like I loved them?"

The fires we walk through have a way of illuminating the

truth in our lives. It wasn't until I began to heal that I realized I needed to break the destructive cycle I had learned. Do you have destructive cycles you have ignored that you need to deal with? Take a minute to reflect. I want to share with you a story where Jesus' disciples learned about breaking cycles. One day Jesus and his disciples were on the mission field in Mark Chapter 9. A child possessed by a demon spirit was experiencing seizures; he was a deaf mute and would foam at the mouth. His father brought the child to the disciples. The child was his father's only son. You can imagine his desperation for his son to be healed. The boy's father explained to Jesus how he had brought his son to his disciples first – but they were unable to cast the demon out of him. Jesus asked the boy's father how long has this been happening to him? The father replied with two words, "From childhood." Jesus casts the unclean spirit out of the boy and returned him to his father delivered and set free. Can you imagine the joy his father felt? Knowing God had broken the destructive cycle and granted him peace from the traumatic events he had suffered. What we experienced as a child (family abuse, trauma or dysfunction) is not beyond God's repair. Have you ever paused to examine how long you have been dealing with destructive cycles of thinking patterns and bad decisions? God is willing and able to break the destructive cycles in our lives. The only thing He requires is that you believe it is possible.

I can only imagine the look on the faces of Jesus' disciples who weren't able to cast out the demon spirits. Finally, they all entered the house and asked Jesus, "Why could we not cast it out?" Jesus simply replied, "This kind can come out by nothing but prayer and fasting." From this Biblical example, I learned that prayer and fasting were spiritual disciplines I needed.

A Biblical fast is when one abstains from eating food and drinking or both for a predetermined time. It is a private, spiritual practice between you and God only. The fast symbolizes a spiritual purpose and has the power to break strongholds.

As I struggled to break destructive cycles in my life I realized that binge eating was a major stronghold for me. I ate when I was happy, sad and even angry. Food became my means of soothing myself. Honestly, I worshiped food. It became a 'god' to me. I know I'm not alone.

As a result of my overeating, in October 2017, I began to experience extremely bad headaches, aching of the eyes and disturbing sleep patterns. I went to the doctor and was diagnosed with high blood pressure. My highest reading was 227/110. My highest weight was 230 pounds. I was obese. I realized I had to shift my mindset in order for me to break the destructive cycle of overeating. Most often we want change to occur from the outside because it somehow seems easier to use external methods. Whether we use shakes, pills or the latest diet fad; it is all superficial. True release must begin within our heart and mind. The body will follow.

One evening while kneeling in prayer, I cried out to God for help. God led me on a 21-day fast. It felt like a journey through the wilderness. However, what I learned during fasting and prayer was that it has the power to bring one's mind into focus so they can confront the real, deep-rooted issues. When we address the root of the matter we can experience true change.

Dealing with my roots allowed me to break the cycle. For years, I lied to myself saying I could stop overeating whenever I desired. In reality, I used food to medicate and numb my hurt and disappointment. My first step to healing, was admitting I had a problem. Denial will only delay our healing. The freedom

I felt in giving myself permission to admit I had a problem was liberating. My next step was to create a list of the emotions that triggered the overeating: anger, hurt, and unforgiveness. Then, I wrote WHY I felt this way: it made me feel better. However, that was a lie. I did not feel better after over eating. I had to replace the lies with the truth. I was trying to accomplish, in my own strength, what God wanted me to ask and rely on Him to help me with.

> *I can do all things through Christ who strengthens me.*
> —PHILIPPIANS 4:13

God's power can destroy whatever is keeping us from true freedom. How many times do we struggle to accomplish in our own self-effort what God is willing to assist us with? I believe Jesus heard my cry for help and faithfully answered my prayers. The 21-day fast was a success. When we want freedom and healing more than food and drink, we will receive it. God used that time to move me from independence to depending upon Him. We will never accomplish true freedom using our own strength. My love for food put me in years of bondage but Jesus gave me complete liberty.

> *Now the Lord is the Spirit; and where the Spirit of the Lord is, there is liberty.*
> —2 CORINTHIANS 3:17 NKJV

We all are at different places in our relationship with God. Some have never fasted and prayed. Others may be veterans at praying and fasting. No matter your spiritual level, God is more than willing to help you. If you begin a fast, get weak and break it, ask God to honor the time you were able to fast. Please do not feel guilty or condemned. This is a spiritual muscle that will need to be built. If you have never fasted and prayed, I encourage you to ask God to teach you the benefits of this spiritual discipline. You will be amazed at how it empowers you to experience greater levels of joy and freedom. Destructive habits you thought were impossible to break will no longer hold you captive. There is nothing more exciting than the feeling of breakthrough.

"Moreover, when you fast, do not be like the hypocrites, with a sad countenance. For they disfigure their faces that they may appear to men to be fasting. Assuredly, I say to you, they have their reward.
~MATTHEW 6:16 KNJV

God loves and desires us to be totally free. He wants us to live a life of complete victory. He has placed unlimited power within us to be bondage-breakers. Chains of destructive habits can no longer hold us. It is possible to break free and never return to destructive cycles. Be encouraged and remember, it is not what we can accomplish in our own strength. It is only when we use the weapons God has given us and rely upon His power, we experience true freedom. With God, all things are possible.

Step 6 – Commit to Prayer and Fasting

Prayer for Fasting

Most Gracious and Heavenly Father, I thank You for teaching me the importance of using my spiritual weapons of prayer and fasting. Thank You for showing me in Your word there are some things in my life that can only be addressed and overcome by prayer and fasting.

As I am led by Your Spirit to fast and pray, I thank You for giving me the grace to begin and end every fast in total obedience. Thank You for the grace to overcome every temptation while praying and fasting. I receive Your grace and I declare it is sufficient for me, in Jesus name. Amen.

Born Out Of The Fire

Confronting Your Bloodline

*Therefore, just as through one man sin entered the
world, and death through sin, and thus death spread to
all me, because all sinned –*

—ROMANS 5: 12 NKJV

G od desires a loving relationship with His beloved creation
that will last forever. God created Adam and Eve, in His
image and set them apart in, the Garden of Eden. It was God's
intention for them to live in the garden under His bountiful
blessings, surrounded by His love. They had everything they
needed from their loving Father. After Adam and Eve dis-
obeyed God and sinned in the garden, without a choice, we
were all born into sin.

Sin is simply missing the mark or falling short of doing what
God asks us in His word. Although Adam and Eve were created
and born perfect, that purity was lost once they ate of the tree God
asked them not to eat of. They were no longer innocent. Their eyes
were open to right and wrong, evil and good. The curse and pun-
ishment God pronounced upon them was more than they could
bear. They would be physically separated from their loving Creator
when He told them they would have to leave. They would no longer be allowed to live in the beautiful Garden of Eden. That curse
was transferred to all born after Adam and Eve.

*...So that he does not corrupt his bloodline among
his people, for I am the Lord who sets him apart.*
—LEVICTICUS 21:15 CSB

In order to identify our bloodline patterns we must be willing to go beyond the surface and dig deep within to heal from family abuse, trauma and dysfunction. When you are ready to embrace change, the destructive bloodline patterns will be released. Your bloodline consists of your direct family line. It includes parents, grandparents and great-grandparents. Every bloodline has established patterns whether good or bad. During my healing and deliverance process, I asked God to show me what was in my family line. When stubborn circumstances would continue to arise, I would pray and ask God, "Where is this coming from? Why do I go through this very same situation every year at this time?" He would answer, "the bloodline." At that moment, I would search God's word and pray scriptures to help me overcome the evil forces that were presenting themselves.

Have you ever felt you were being attacked by one thing after the other? Every time you try and catch your footing from one setback another one delivers a blow causing you to feel overwhelmed. I honestly did not know how God wanted me to pray for my family bloodline. I thank the Holy Spirit for being the greatest Teacher I have ever known.

While in prayer one day, God said to me, "You are the bloodline breaker." I had no idea what God was referring to. I have a funny sense of humor with God. My response was, "Is that like being the line leader like in kindergarten?" I literally could not stop laughing at myself. Honestly it felt good to laugh after years of unbearable pain. I encourage you to take time often to just laugh.

You are on your way out! Your freedom and deliverance are just over the horizon! You will laugh again! You will love again! You will shine again! You will dream again! You will dance again! Your hope is being restored! I prophesy to you that you will be the last one laughing. What God was showing me was teaching me to confront destructive patterns of my bloodline. This was to ensure that future generations would not have to suffer what previous generations suffered.

I would like to share a story with you. In the Bible, in the Book of Esther, Queen Esther was an example of courage and bravery. The story unfolds to show us that Esther's disappointing childhood paled in comparison to the amazing future God planned for her. She became an orphan after her parents died and her Uncle Mordecai adopted and raised her. Esther was a Jew and her Uncle asked her not to disclose her nationality to anyone. There came a time when King Xerxes dethroned his previous Queen Vashti for dishonoring one of his requests. The king then began a nationwide search for his new queen. Esther, along with several other virgins were taken into King Xerxes' harem and trained for a life of royalty if selected by the king. When Esther went before the king, he immediately found her to be the most beautiful of all the women and chose her as Queen, placing the royal crown on her head.

Haman was one of the king's highest nobles and he hated Mordecai because he was a Jew and Mordecai refused to bow in Haman's presence. This infuriated Haman and he then plotted to have all the Jews killed, especially Mordecai. Haman deceitfully convinced King Xerxes' to have all the Jews in the region killed. The king ignorantly agreed and set a date for the execution of all the Jews. Mordecai informed Esther of Haman's wicked plot and begged her to let the king know. Queen Esther then embarked on three days and nights of prayer and fasting. Once granted access to the king's presence, she would now disclose to the king that she was a Jew. As his wife, she would be included in this annihilation of the Jews. It had been 30 days since the King had requested Queen Esther to come into his presence. And she risked death by entering the King's presence uninvited.

"Go and gather together all the Jews of Susa and fast for me. Do not eat or drink for three days, night or day. My maids and I will do the same. And then, though it is against the law, I will go in to see the king. If I must die, I must die."
—ESTHER 4:16 NLT

After Queen Esther ended her prayer and fasting, she entered the royal court of the king unauthorized. The king was not at all angry with Esther but rather asked her what she wanted. He would grant it to her, even up to half his kingdom! Instead of blurting out her request to save her and her people; Esther planned and prepared a banquet and invited the King. Esther also invited Haman to the banquet. At the banquet, Esther revealed her nationality to the king and explained to the king that Haman was behind the wicked plan to have the Jews killed for money. This would mean, as his wife, she had to die as well. This infuriated the king. He ordered Haman and his entire family to be killed. Queen Esther and Mordecai was given Haman's entire state by the king. Esther so loved the next generation she was willing to risk her life, pray, fast and go before the king.

Is it possible you are the BLOODLINE BREAKER for your family? Have you endured harsh tests and trials? God uses many of our circumstances to shape our character and prepare us to help and serve others. Could it be God called you to bring positive change in your family line?

I lost my father at the age of 65 to congestive heart failure. At the age of 42 my mother died of HIV/AIDS. At the age of 23 God gave me the courage to survive the fire of a domestically abusive relationship. Satan is a liar and a deceiver. He plants thoughts in our minds that are not true. He leads us to believe we will never defeat the patterns of our bloodline and remain enslaved to our family's line of negative behaviors. You see my bloodline was plagued with overeating, depression, need for approval, drug use, domestic violence and so much more "Yet Still I Rise." God's word has the power to destroy bloodlines.

I am so grateful that my children did not suffer from a broken home, family abuse, trauma or dysfunction. Our family is close-knit. When the waves of life come crashing in unexpectedly, we pray together and for one another. I didn't experience this type of love and respect growing up. I have great peace knowing God gave my family the tools to love and communicate In a healthier way.

I learned the purpose of the fire was to purify and not consume me. It increased my capacity to handle difficult tests and trials. It built my spiritual stamina. It taught me endurance. It taught me mercy and compassion for other's sufferings. The fire taught me to rise up, confront and conquer. We will never conquer what we are unwilling to confront.

I would like to share a prayer that blessed me during a season when I needed it most. This prayer allowed me to see change in my life; I pray it helps you and your family as it helped mine.

Bloodline Prayer – Unknown Author

Heavenly Father, I repent and ask for Your forgiveness in the name of Jesus for my sins of breaking your first and second commandments, and I also repent and ask for forgiveness for any sins, transgressions, and iniquities that may have been passed down to me through my bloodline, especially the sins of making an idol out of the things You created, and worshiping these things rather than You, the Creator.

Father, I ask for Your forgiveness for my family line and for anyone in my generational bloodline linked to me that has committed this sin and chosen to serve other gods or worship them. I pray that You will forgive us and cleanse me/my children/grandchildren etc. of my/our iniquities and sins because I/we know that I/we have broken the first and the second commandment which is an act of disobedience to You.

I ask that the blood of the Lamb of God will cleanse and purify me/children, grandchildren, etc. from this sin and cleanse me/us from every negative impact that this sin may have brought into my life/our lives in Jesus name. You said that if we confess our sins, You are faithful and just to forgive us and cleanse us from all our unrighteousness (1 John 1:9).

Heavenly Father, by the authority given to me in the name of Jesus Christ, I now break myself/children/grandchildren etc. free from every vow and all evil agreements that were made on my/our behalf and sever myself/children/grandchildren etc. from these covenants and vows. I declare that I/we will not be a partaker and will not participate in such agreements or vows as from this day. I destroy every effect of these covenants in my life/our lives in Jesus name.

I now confess and receive Your blessings, promised in Deuteronomy 28:1-14 over my life/children/grandchildren/lineage in Jesus name. Whoever the Son sets free is free indeed. I seal my prayers with the Blood of Jesus. Amen.

The good news is once we receive Jesus as our Lord and Savior, we are born into a new family; the family of God. I thank God for sending His son Jesus to break all curses from our family's bloodline.

Step 7 – Commit to Confrontation

Prayer for Boldness:

Dear Heavenly Father, I come to You through the power of the blood of Your Son Jesus asking You for the boldness to confront the destructive forces, patterns, curses and behaviors in my bloodline. I ask for Your divine wisdom to open my eyes to see and my ears to hear every secret concerning my bloodline.

Father God, Your scripture declares in Proverbs 28:1 that the righteous is as bold as a lion. Grant me the confidence to stand in the face of opposition and wage war by the authority of Your Spirit. I thank You for the victory and blessings that flow through our bloodlines now and forevermore, in Jesus name. Amen.

Born Out Of The Fire

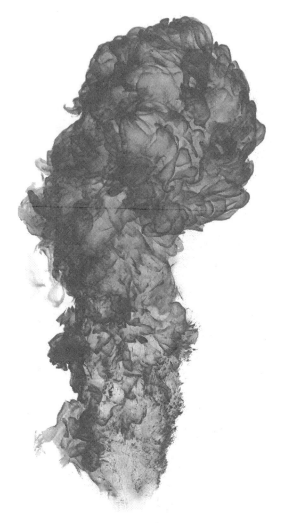

My Journey Through The Fire

I want to thank you for taking this journey with me through the fire. Transparency is a vital key to our freedom. And in return, God gets the glory for His miracle working power in our lives. The woman you see today no longer lives with the regret and shame of her past.

I sincerely believe no one is exempt from walking through the "fiery trials" of this life. Through the fire came the birth of my story and my life's purpose. I was born to be a deliverer. I was born to be a voice for the voiceless. I was born a champion for the weak. I emerged from Trauma To Triumph. I emerged from family abuse to God's favor. I emerged from dysfunction to defeating the plans of the enemy for my life. So, will you! If you are willing to...

Commit to Forgive
Commit to Healing
Commit to Unselfishness
Commit to Make a Decision
Commit to Asking for Help
Commit to Prayer and Fasting
Commit to Confrontation

God used the pain of my past to create a testimony within me to share with others. I praise God for every fiery trial He brought me through! As you walk through the fire of life, remember the fire was never meant to destroy you, but to make you stronger so that you can bless someone else. Rise up and step into your purpose. The world is waiting for you to show up. You have been Born Out Of The Fire!

God Bless You!

Made in the USA
Middletown, DE
18 May 2019